The Scribes of Osiris

The Mirrors Of Truth

by

George Mendoza

Other Books By George Mendoza and James Nathan Post:

SPIRIT MAN
A Vision Of Courage

Other Books From The Scribes Of Osiris:

Sedona Esoterica -- Dowsing / I Ching / Candles
The Stone Vessel Of Saqqara

www.georgemendoza.com
www.postpubco.com

THE MIRRORS OF TRUTH

By George Mendoza

ACKNOWLEDGMENT:

I hope it can be said this little book is inspirational, and makes people feel good about themselves and each other, in the way that my mother Cindy is a continual inspiration to me. She will always be first among all of the heroes of my life.

I hope my beloved Estella can somehow appreciate how much I appreciate the years of support, companionship and love which she contributed to my life, and to this book, and how much I hope and pray for her happiness always.

I hope I can express how much I appreciate the editorial and creative participation of my friend of so many years, James Nathan Post, my word wizard who has stood through many long dark and dry times like Merlin at my side, as we have created some very fine enchantments and spells, and cast them upon the ether.

The Scribes Of Osiris is an ancient order of arts and letters, founded by the scribe Aenosar, charioteer in the wars against Assyria, student of the works of Master Imhotep, architect, engineer, philosopher, and scribe. Aenosar spent his life without follower, slave, or employee, working as a common scribe by day, each night dragging one more stone one step closer to the temple he was building in the desert, and engraving each with his acknowledgment that the Eternally Conscious God is the author of all that is wise and beautiful and true.

In 1973, in a converted chicken coop in Sebastopol, James Nathan Post discovered Aenosar's temple on a para-sentient investigation. In the decades since, he has worked tirelessly to create a virtual facsimile of that temple, built only of the etherial winds of the internet, and inscribed on a few ephemeral bits of papyrus, in the vast wilderness of 21st Century American literature.

George Mendoza, aspiring novelist and screenwriter, became associated with The Scribes Of Osiris in 1981, one of the first artists whose talent and desire to create meaningful literary work was recognized by the order.

Alex St. Luc
Aen Osar Emeritus

INTRODUCTION:

In many of my dreams, and in my dream worlds where I wander as Spirit Man, I am often confronted with the image of the mirror as a tool of truth. I hope that doesn't mean I am obsessed with looking at myself, though I do believe that we mortal souls can learn the most about our immortal nature, and the One who is Father to us all, by looking closely at ourselves. Maybe it just comes of being impressed when I was very young by the talking mirror in Snow White, that always told the truth, whether you wanted to hear it or not. What a powerful and frightening thing such an oracle would be. How many of us would ever look into that mirror at all, much less ask it a question?

When I began to lose my vision as a young man, mirrors took on a terrible new meaning. Those who are totally blind say they have no sensation at all of seeing anything. "It looks just like trying to see with your foot," a friend once told me. My vision is still a very full experience, but it is a distorted and surreal experience, garish, glaring, like the flashes of color you see with your eyes closed, but bright as daylight. Sometimes it looks like the world has been scooped up like blobs of bright paint, and splattered in my face.

You might well imagine that looking into a mirror with such vision would be a very strange experience indeed, and you would be right. But that experience taught me something. Like the use of psychedelics, which distort the perception in bizarre and radical ways, the horror of my newly acquired blindness began to teach me how dependent we are on our habitual perceptions for our sense of security in the world, and in time. Statements like, "I trust what I can see with my own two eyes," take on a very different meaning. I began to ask myself how much else around me I was taking for granted I could see clearly, and thought I knew.

I began to ask myself how much of what I thought I knew about myself was the result of what I was seeing in other such mirrors around me, distorted or not, and how much was the result of deliberately not looking at some of the other mirrors around me. I started looking at the whole world as a hall of mirrors, each one offering me the opportunity to see myself from a new viewpoint, whether I liked what I saw or not.

For me, one of the most important kinds of such mirrors is the act of creativity. The act of painting or writing or speaking to people is like putting mirror images of yourself out into the world so you can see them. When you write a book, or paint a picture, or for that matter, whatever you create in the world, you are then able to see yourself, or at least a reflection of yourself. It is in a way like going looking for the talking mirrors, and then publishing what they say. You have to live with what you do, and with what you see, but you can't be accused of not looking. The less distortion you create, that is, the more honestly your mirror images reflect the truth, the better you can come to know yourself, and thereby hopefully come to know a little bit more about your place in the eternal context of things. That is, after all, the thing we all would most highly value in our hearts to know.

One of the things I have discovered in the course of

the years we have spent writing about Spirit Man is this: the most important thing about discovering that you are Spirit Man is discovering that the most important thing about being Spirit Man is helping somebody else discover that he is his own Spirit Man, and he has all the time and all the universes there are to imagine and explore. How do you do that? Easy. You learn to become a mirror, and you do your best to help other people see in you how beautiful they are themselves.

CHAPTER 1: THE FIRST MIRROR

"Look into your own heart first!"

The truth is we are all blind to tomorrow. Nobody knows what tomorrow will bring. Nobody has the answers. Most of the time, we don't even have the questions. After my uncle died, I climbed up the mountain in the barren deserts of southern New Mexico in early August. I sat down on top of the lone dome shaped mountain named Tortugas, which means turtle in Spanish. Tortugas is located in the middle of nowhere, which is just where I like to be. I was thinking about life and pondering the mysteries of the world.

To the east I see the Organ Mountains, one big dinosaur toothed jawbone sticking up out of the middle of the desert. To the west is the Mesilla Valley. What I see is a haze of brown and green, but I know from my travels there that the valley is full of groves of pecan trees, fields of cotton, green chile, and corn. The Rio Grande runs through the heart of the valley. There are stands of cottonwood trees and big tangles of Salt Cedar. You know, I am legally blind, but that does not mean I can't see. In my mind's eye, I see all of life unfolding before me. A truck driver falls asleep at the wheel and ploughs into the car in front of him. A little boy is in a field playing with a BB gun. He is stooped over a robin, wondering why he shot it. A man is beating his dog. His screams of anger echo throughout the woods.

"This is the condition of life," says the Spirit Man. "The condition of suffering. We can dream of a better tomorrow, but this is what we have to live with today."

The world knows me as George Mendoza, but I am Sebastian Spirit Man. I am a pilgrim.

I am wondering about evil in the world. I am wishing for a world of peace and love, a paradise in our minds. Think about this! What kind of world do we live in? How can the world be full of such beauty and so much suffering at the same time? The human struggle, it seems to me, is a weird experiment on a grand scale. Sometimes I think the world is in pain, but I cannot feel it.

I am a Pilgrim on a journey. My eyes today see a world where evil seems to outweigh good. What do you see through your own eyes? It is a constant struggle to see through my eyes. But is it any different for you?

When I was fifteen years old, a rare eye disease took my eyesight away from me. That was a very cruel thing for me to experience at such a formative age. I lost my eyesight, but I gained a special kind of vision. I think that is why I am sitting on top of this mountain, asking these questions.

I love it here in New Mexico. This is where I have been since I was seventeen. This is where I live and breathe and see my beautiful visions and dream out my dreams. The light here is a clear light. When I came here from New York City, I found that this sunlight made me feel good. It gave me energy. It helped me see. I could see so well that I started to run in the desert. I found a special place. It is a rock shelter on top of this mountain that looks out over the Mesilla Valley. I have a special friend here. My friend is made of pure light and spirit. I have been here many times before to seek a better understanding of the secrets of the heart and the mysteries of the world. I think I will sit here in the cool shade beside the rock wall for the rest of the day.

This book was given to me by The Great Spirit who moves like the wind around all of us. Some call The Great Spirit God, which is fine by me. Call The Great Spirit whatever you want. No matter to me. I have given the Great Spirit a name. I call my Great Spirit The Dream Child. The Dream Child is neither a dream nor a child. The Dream Child is neither male nor female. The Dream Child is a vision. The Dream Child appears to me whenever I choose to see it. When the Dream Child needs to tell me something very important, it speaks to me in a dream. "This is what I ask of you, oh Spirit of Man," the Great Spirit would boom out to me like a peal of thunder. "Teach others what you learn from me, while you sit here on top of the mountain!"

I smile. What could a blind man sitting on top of a mountain in the desert expect to teach to anyone?

On this day you and I will meet The Dream Child and learn as much as we can. On this day, it is time for us to see the light and get out of the darkness. On this day, it is time to look into the mirrors of truth and not be blinded by lies and half-truths.

The wind blows gently across the mountaintop. I feel its hot dry kiss on my cheek. I smell the creosote, and a hint of brush burning down in the valley. I taste the dry heat of the midday sun soaking into the desert floor far below. I cannot see the wind, but I know it is there. What is the nature of truth? Was man born innocent and good, and later came to evil? When a child is born, we accept this genesis of innocence. But is this a truth for all of mankind? I cannot see the truth. I cannot touch it, cannot smell it, cannot taste it. And yet I am always looking for it. I am a pilgrim on a journey. There are questions at every turn. But where are the answers?

I have a very wise friend named Tokind (he says it's too-kind) who doesn't believe in a God who looks like an old man with a flowing white beard. Tokind is a pronoid. A pronoid is the opposite of a paranoid, someone who believes the universe is a vast conspiracy against him. "I believe that the universe is a vast conspiracy to do me good," he says. "I think the so-called truth is a dangerous trap. People who claim the truth either end up doing great evil, or get themselves crucified. The journey is the thing! Don't know where I heard it, but I believe it." I met Tokind six years ago when I was looking for someone to help me do a web site. He's some kind of wizard, I found out, when it comes to that.

There is a little monument about three hundred feet from where I sit. It is a simple pile of rocks, painted white, with a cross on top. It is a shrine to the Virgin of Guadalupe. Every year on the 12th of December, the people of the little village of Tortugas below gather together their friends, family, and palm fronds shipped special from California. They climb the mountain, a trip of several miles, some of them barefoot, carrying candles against the cold December night. At the top of the mountain they build a huge fire and they pray to the Virgin. The shrine is a modest monument, a place where they all will meet, at a certain time, for a certain reason.

I am Spirit Man. Truth is precious to me. I have my

own truths, and you cannot take them away from me. I understand that you too, have your truths. I wouldn't dream of trying to take them away. We must all share our truths, because we are all a part of some greater truth. We must all look into our own hearts, and share the truths that we find there.

My uncle, Wallace Von Spirit Man, insisted he was an Atheist. He said he did not believe that there was a God because there was too much suffering and pain in the world. Wallace worked as an art director at Universal Studios in California for many years. He was a cartoon artist and inventor. I spent time with him in California for several years, when he was sick. One night at the dinner table he pulled out his sketchpad. He showed me his designs for a special pair of eyeglasses to help me see. Wallace was dying of cancer. I looked through his notebook, page after page of eyeglasses. They were rings of prisms. He had been working on these designs for several years. He wanted me to see.

As a young man, Wallace was a lifeguard at Zuma beach in California during the long hot summer months. He told me many stories about people he saved from drowning in the ocean. He insisted that I should learn to be a good swimmer. And thanks to him, I am! Wallace would build these movie sets with crews of artists like him. They would build sets for ancient cities, westerns, urban dramas... you name it. He worked on a huge golden Pyramid for a TV production called "Gold Monkey." He was always very disappointed that the movie was shot but never aired. "It's like I create worlds and then watch them get put on a shelf," he said.

That idea has never left me. Wallace worked hard at making worlds. Maybe he wanted this world to be a better place. He insisted he was an Atheist, but he was really angry with God. On his deathbed, he told me something that I will never forget. "Man created God out of need, and not the other way around." I had never thought of it exactly that way. In some strange way, it made sense to me. God does not need us! No, we need God more than He needs us! Wallace slipped into a coma for several weeks before he died. My aunt Linda told me that she was reading an article in the newspaper to him when suddenly he opened up his eyes, looked straight up to heaven, and let out his last breath.

"Was there a hint of him believing in God, since he was so close to death? I don't know," says the Spirit Man. "Do you think that Wallace needed a sign from God? What kind of sign do you need?"

The day Wallace died I heard a loud crash in the spare bedroom. I found the shards of a broken mirror that had fallen off the wall. Is the truth like a perfect mirror? Look at the shards of the broken mirror on the floor. You see the pieces, and you know that what you are looking at was once a mirror. The Spirit Man says, "As a pilgrim, I am seeking that perfect mirror. The shards are all around me. I just have to put them back together."

Once I visited my cousin, Ralphie Spirit Man, who lives in Artesia, New Mexico, with his wife and five children. Three out of his five children were born mentally retarded. "There's oil in our drinking water," he said. "Have a taste. You'll see what I mean." I gave him a puzzled look and took a sip from the cup he offered me. It tasted weird and slimy and it felt slick going down my throat.

"Is this true?" I asked my red-bearded cousin.

Ralphie nodded. "Why do you think my children are retarded?"

We sat down on Ralphie's front porch with some beers and visited for the rest of the day. I wondered why Ralphie was not upset about his situation in life. He told me that he had found Jesus, and that he was not worried about anything. "With Christ as my personal savior, I know where I am going."

It had been a very hot still day. That night, I slept on his front porch. I had a very strange dream. I dreamed that everybody in the whole wide world had suddenly become mentally retarded just like Ralphie's kids. I walked through a big crowd of people. I noticed that everyone was standing around, clapping their hands, and babbling. Some were seated cross-legged on the ground, rocking back and forth and humming, but there was no melody. I didn't know where to stand. I didn't know what to think or say. Then I saw my friend, Joseph, a retarded boy. I see him every Wednesday afternoon at my art class. In my dream, he was a fat boy who was talking wildly on his cell phone. He held it upside down to his right ear. He was not looking at me. He kept repeating over and over, "I love you! I love you! Kiss! Kiss! Kiss!" For just one moment, suspended in time, the whole wide world was full of peace and love. The retarded boy spoke only of one thing: Love.

What was the Great Spirit saying to me? Are we too smart to practice peace and love? Love is why we are here. In my dream I saw no hate, no aggression, only bliss.

Because the whole world had become mentally retarded for a while, there was no hate in anyone's heart and no thought of war or violence against any living thing. "Is this the perfect mirror?" asked the Spirit Man.

My cousin Ralphie lost his mind to religion. Recently, I got a phone call from his wife. She told me that he went crazy. He lost his job, they lost their home too, and they had to file bankruptcy.   All of this because he loved Jesus too much, she told me. He denied all of his responsibilities in this world. I listened to her and tried to comfort her. When our conversation was over I cried for my cousin and then I went out in the desert for a long walk. The real truth is that I am a Believer but I don't know what to believe in anymore. Sometimes I wonder if I believe in anything. What should I believe in? Should I believe in God? Should I believe in love?

Take a look at the world around you and me. Look how it really is. We are in the middle of World War III. Who is God? Where is God these days? What is God? At one time in my life, I thought that sorrow and pain could actually teach us a lesson in life that would make us stronger and better. Now, I am not so sure about this. I have seen so much through these blind eyes of mine! I have seen so many people go through very painful situations in their lives. My uncle Wallace lost his battle to cancer and Ralphie went insane. The pain that I saw them endure was too much for them to overcome. It weighed them down and tore them apart. Their mirrors shattered.

Do you understand what the Spirit Man is trying to tell you? You own a piece of the mirror. We all have the power within ourselves to be the sons and daughters of

God. Tokind likes to quote Stewart Brand: "We are as gods, and may as well get good at it." If we fill our hearts with love then we can become God-like. If we turn our minds away from hatred and anger, imagine what kind of world would we see. There is a fine line between darkness and light. Pain and pleasure. Day and night. Angels and demons. Questions and answers. Life and death.

Now listen to me! Blood runs through our veins like a river of life. My blood is red and so is yours. We are black and red and yellow and white, and all of our mirrors reflect the same pure light. We all live under the same blue sky and walk upon the same dark brown earth and drink from the same fountain of healing waters and breathe the same air. The real truth is that we all live between the sky and earth. What is between the sky and earth is us. We should be dancing upon the earth and filling it up with sounds of sweet music.

Up here, in my mind's eye, I see life unfolding before me once again. I see the truck driver killing the family in the car in front of him. He made a mistake. I see the little boy with his BB gun crying over a dead bird. He didn't think about the consequences of firing that shot. I see the angry man crying over the dog he has just beaten to death. He really loved that dog. He was trying to beat himself up. I see my uncle Wallace trying to save the world. He was demanding an answer from God. I see my cousin Ralphie, blissfully watching his world fall apart all around him. He only waits for The Rapture. That never comes.

The DREAM CHILD: "We must all look into our hearts and share the truths that we find there. If you would save another's heart, you must look into your own heart first. You must share what you find there. Whatever you see in the first mirror of truth you must embrace. We all live and die, laugh and cry, fail and try, by our own hearts. Sebastian Spirit Man! Listen to me! This is The Dream Child speaking to you! Close your eyes now and tell me what you see! The Mirrors of Truth will set you freeeeee!

I am a fruit! I love the taste of a mouth-watering mango especially the ones from Old Mexico on a hot summer day! I am the fruit of my mother and father. Cindy Huber was born in Manhattan but she grew up near Charon, Massachusetts, on a small farm with her parents and her brother Wallace. Cindy and Wallace used to fish in a small pond in their back yard. My mother was and still is a very pretty woman. She loved acting, and studied drama in high school. My mother is a butterfly. She loves the company of other people. Her laughter is welcome in any group. She loves people, and she is committed to improving the lives of people who cannot necessarily speak up for themselves. Cindy Huber has always lived like this.

There is another George Mendoza, living in New York. He is my Father. I am his first born son. I have only met him twice in my entire life, once when I was nine, and a second time when I was nineteen years old. I have talked with him a handful of times on the telephone. I can only remember receiving two letters from him. All of these communications were about me approaching him for some kind of relationship, and him warning me away.

I was born on April Fools Day in 1955, on Governor's Island, New York. Cindy was twenty-six years old, and

George was nineteen. My mother told me that one morning when I was two months old this man named George told her that he was going out to buy a newspaper. He never came back. Cindy was faced with being both mother and father to me. I am sure that this was a terrifying thing for her to face. But I sure didn't know it. My childhood was like a Disneyland fantasy. I grew up in Manhattan. Every weekend my mother and I would visit the Garden of Eden. She told me that Central Park was the Garden of Eden, and you could not have convinced me otherwise. The place was magical to me. I remember catching frogs and turtles, and feeding the squirrels out of my hand. I remember collecting buckets of Indian arrowheads. I remember seeing the sunlight filtering through the tall trees and dancing upon the ground all around us. I must have been four or five years old one Saturday morning when mom and I walked down a stony path underneath the giant trees. It was cloudy and a chilly breeze stung my skin. I stopped short, looking up at those dark imposing giants. Mom scooped me up in her arms, and then suddenly the clouds parted. I counted seven rays of the sun shining down through those trees.

We lived in Manhattan until I was five years old. What I remember the most about New York City were the tall buildings, the dinosaurs at the museums, and of course the Garden of Eden. Central park divides the city right down the middle, the east side from the west side. My mother would always tell me, "Paradise is in our minds and hearts, Georgie! You have to make the most of what you have been given!" Everybody knows there are rats the size of cats in New York City. I was the child of a single parent in the city that people think of when they hear the word city. I might have been sitting on the floor of a dark cold apartment, watching cold images on a black and white TV. This was not the life that my dearest friend and mother chose for me. My mother had the wisdom to show me the fruit of the Garden of Eden.

When I was six years old, my mother and I moved to a quaint town named Stonybrook on the northern shores of Long Island. Two hours by train from New York City, Stonybrook was another paradise. Living there meant that the woods, the beach, the cries of seagulls in the salty Atlantic air, were never more than a stones throw away. I loved it there! As a boy, I walked through the swamps hunting for sting rays and sea turtles and horseshoe crabs and fish. I ran up and down the sandy bluffs and walked along the beaches all day long until I was sure I was lost. I remember that feeling of being lost. It was a fantasy, really, because I always knew where the shore was. The shore would lead me back home. But that feeling of being lost was special to me. That sense of adventure, that feeling of being on my own, is where I truly found myself!

I always came home to my mother, my Uncles Bob and Wallace, and my Grandparents, to a place where I was loved deeply and without question. School was fun. It was where I found good friends like Bobby Cook and Neal Hidalgo. They are still friends of mine today. My uncles Bob and Wallace would take me fishing for striped bass and bluefish. We always caught something. My uncles taught me how to find, catch, and clean a fish. We ate like kings.

Neal and Bobby and I went to summer camps,

19

trekked through the woods, and swam all day in the ocean or in lake Ronkonkama. We played baseball, basketball, football, ice hockey, and competed in track and field events in school. I was at home in school too. I was an honor-roll student, and I was surrounded by kids and teachers who appreciated me for who I was. I never felt alone.

When I was nine years old, I remember a terrifying dream. I was running through the woods alone. A fog was all around me. I was very afraid, of what I do not know. The branches cut my face as I crashed through the woods. I stumbled in the darkness. I could not see anything in front of me at all. I was all alone. In the darkness I screamed out, "I'm going blind, I'm going blind, I'm going blind."

CHAPTER 2: THE SECOND MIRROR

"To find the truth, you must draw blood!"

The truth is if you and I were to switch eyeballs for just fifteen minutes, you'd probably go crazy. Objects dance. Take a vase. As it floats through space in front of your eyes, its ghostly silhouette emits contrails of colors. You'd also see pinwheels, zigzags, trapezoids, lightning bolts, and rays of the sun spinning. You'd see the moon turning into blood, and snow blowing black. The next minute you're whisked to a discotheque-like atmosphere with a strobe light show. Then brilliant, dazzling lights flare crazily back and forth and fountains of colors explode like fireworks. You look down a three-foot tunnel through imaginary straws and see a kaleidoscope of images. Look at your hand. There are at least thirty eyeballs on the palm of your hand. Then everywhere you stare, hundreds of eyeballs are watching you.

This all happens in your central vision from the tip of your nose to about three feet in front of your face. Beyond three feet everything goes to gray snow. It's no man's land out there - a kind of limbo.

I don't know why I got this rare eye disease. It may be hard to believe, but I wouldn't trade my eyeballs for a healthy set of eyes even for a second. Even though I've been to hell with this blindness, when I peel my layers of fear away like peeling the outer tough layers of an onion, my blindness is actually a blessing. Without my vision I would be painting the stuff everyone else does – the cactus in the foreground, the sky in the background. Instead I see shimmering bolts of blue energy flying through the air and fiery balls of sunlight exploding on the canvas. Artistically I'm a visually impaired cross between Vincent Van Gogh and Claude Monet.

Now I can say I have it all. I have a meaningful life, and Beautiful Estella who is my true love. I have great friends, gourmet food, adventure, and a computer that talks to me. I even have a unique way of "seeing." I didn't always feel this way.

There were no mountains for me in Stonybrook, New York. I was fifteen years old, an honor roll student, and a star athlete. I was surrounded by friends who would cheer for me when I shined on the basketball court. But I was starting to think that something was wrong. The last half of my ninth grade basketball season had not been going very well. Now we were in the final game. I was on the floor and I had reached out to snatch that ball from its journey down court. Instead, that ball smacked me in the face. Blood was flowing down my chin, and my friends were booing me from the stands. I looked over to my Mom in the stands and I saw her hand go to her mouth in shock. Then I couldn't see anything. Later on in the game I went for a lay-up and got fowled. On the free throw line, the backboard was swaying in and out of my vision. Everything was blurred. The whole scene was swirling around my head. I felt like I was going to pass out, but I knew I couldn't. Everyone was counting on me. I had to make this shot. There were two shots and I missed both of them. We lost the game. The coach came over to me and asked me what was wrong. "I don't know," I told him. "I guess I'm kinda tired." He told me that I had been dropping the ball a lot lately. "Maybe you should get your eyes checked," he said. The disgust in his voice was obvious.

Mom and I drove home from the game in silence. She could tell that I really didn't want to talk about it at that moment. I was sore from the ball bouncing off my face, but my heart was sore for my miserable failure on the court. I had let everyone down. When mom and I got home I went straight to my room and quietly closed the door. I closed my eyes and laid on my bed in the darkness. Mom called me a while later. She asked me to come for dinner. There was a plate on the table where I sat down. I looked down at the plate but something was very wrong. I could see the green leaves of a salad, but the middle of the plate was swimming with black and blood-red. It looked like a bird had been ripped open and laid on a bed of lettuce. "What's this red stuff on the lettuce?" I asked my mom.

"It's a salad, Georgie," she said as she leaned over to look at my plate. "What do you see?"

I screamed back at her, "It looks like a plate full of bloody garbage." I jumped up and stormed back to my room. I slammed the door behind me. Once again I laid down on my bed in darkness.

When I woke up, I was in a dark cool place. Dim light filtered down from above me. All was silence and I was alone. The cold damp walls of the snake pit surrounded me. The snake pit is a spooky place under a bridge where my friends and I would go to talk and tell stories in private. But now I was alone, and I could not see a way to get out of there. The pain in my face and the pain in my heart is all that I can feel. I noticed a glimmer on the floor of the pit. It looked like a shard of broken glass. I reached down to pick it up, and I could see the dim light from above reflected in this fragment of mirror. I cursed myself as I cut my fingers on the shard. The blood flowed down my fingers and dripped to the ground. I begin to cry, and tears flowed down my sore frightened face, and sting my broken lip.

Then I heard my mothers sweet voice, "Georgie, wake up. We have to go see someone."

Over the next few weeks my Mother took me to see a bunch of different doctors. Some seemed to think I had cancer, but none of them could find anything wrong with me. I was getting sicker. I was getting bad headaches. I would see blinding flashes of light that were so painful that I would almost fall to my knees. I was feeling tired all of the time. Some days I would just stay in bed all day.

One day I was a promising young man at the top of his game. The next day I was a sick and frightened boy clinging to his mother's hand on a terrible journey to some unknown dark place.

Finally a doctor at a hospital in Manhattan looked into my eyes and saw something the other doctors had missed. He saw lesions on the back of my eyeballs. He thought he knew what this was, but he told us that it was very rare. Dr. Rosen told us it was fundis flavi maculitus, a hereditary eye disease. He explained to my mother as gently as possible that there was no treatment, no cure. Stunned, my mom and I left the hospital.

As the darkness closed in around me, my world collapsed to the size of my frightened bleeding heart. I had no hope. My athletic career was over. Most of my so-called friends abandoned me. I felt nothing but the

24

darkness all around. I was numb. I lay on darkness of my room, dead to the world. I was in the pit of darkness and I could see no way out.

Then I heard a gentle knock on my bedroom door. My mothers sweet voice called to me. "Georgie, we need to talk". Over the next eighteen months my mother planned our move to a new life in New Mexico, where there was a special school for the blind. I didn't want to go, but I wanted to go. I wanted to fight for what I had in Stonybrook, but in my heart I knew that I could never win those things back. My mother was offering me a new path and I was going to have to trust her.

It took Mom and me two weeks to drive across the Great Plains to the Land of Enchantment. The great flat expanse of the Midwest did not make much of an impression on me. I was mostly worried about where we were going. I slept a lot in the back of the car. Mom listened to radio for company. The music on the radio changed as we drove west. There were only country and western stations out there. I was growing up on the Beatles and the Rolling Stones, but all of this music was about broken hearts, broken dreams, and bad luck. These were three things that I could relate to my life.

Again I heard my mothers sweet voice, calling me over the hum of the motor. "Georgie, wake up, we are in New Mexico." I sat up and rubbed the sleep out of my eyes. I looked out the window and I could see a ring of mountains all around us. The sun was shining bright blue-white on this vast, dreamy landscape. There might not have been any mountains in Stonybrook, but here there were mountains everywhere. As we climbed up a steep mountain pass, and then down the other side into a forest of tall straight trees, I rolled down the window and smelled the fresh pine. We plunged into a tunnel and everything went dark. As we broke out of the other end of the tunnel, I saw and endless expanse of canyon before us, and far off in the distance a shimmering sea of pure white light. This was my welcome to New Mexico.

We found our way to Las Cruces, to our new home.

In the fall of 1972 my mother enrolled my in The New Mexico School for the Visually Handicapped. The school is 70 miles away, in Alamogordo. That town is named for it's huge shady cottonwood trees. I was scared at the idea of being separated from my mother. I was afraid that I was being placed in an institution. When my mother kissed me goodbye and walked back to the car, I was overcome by a deep feeling of loneliness. I felt like I was being abandoned. I had been torn away from my Garden of Eden and dropped into this strange desert. I walked along a straight concrete path to room, closed the door, and threw myself onto the bed. Again, alone in the darkness I wondered what would become of me.

The knock on the door was a load banging sound. This was not my mother's gentle knock. I sat bolt upright on the bed and hollered, "Who is it?"

"My name is T. G. Gibbs," came the answer. I opened the door and asked this T. G. Gibbs what the hell he wanted. Looking off to one side to get the light just right, I could see his tall slim frame with a floppy cowboy hat on top of his head. He spoke with a Texas drawl.

"I saw you slinking over here with your tail between your legs. It looks like you could use a friend." He said.

26

"I want to be left the hell alone!" I said.

"Slim chance of that partner," he snapped back at me. I slammed the door in his face. But he was not going to leave it at that. Everywhere I went on campus, T.G. would appear, to taunt me. "Hey cowboy, have you joined the track and wrestling teams yet?" "Hey sport, I know some sweet young things that want to snuggle up to you." I couldn't ignore him. In the cafeteria he would walk right up and slam his tray down next to me. He insisted on telling me stories about places that he had traveled. He didn't seem to care if I was listening or not. He kept telling me he was going to take me to this place, this church way up north, called Chimayo.

During that year at school I became an Athlete again. I was wrestling and running, and I could hear people cheering for me again when I raced. T.G was the manager of the track and wrestling teams. He was always there to slap my up side the head if slacked off. T.G. would take me out into the desert to run on the weekends. I was training to be a marathon runner. The desert around Alamogordo is full of mesquite and cactus, covered with sharp spines. Some days I would come home with blood running down my legs. It didn't matter. I was going somewhere again.

A year later, in the summer of 1973, my best friend and I awoke hung over from a night of drinking, dancing, and singing. We had just graduated from school and had stayed up all night celebrating. T. G. and I had plans for that day. Our backpacks had been packed a week, ready for a journey north to Chimayo, New Mexico. We were going to hitchhike over three hundred miles to this special place that T. G. would never shut up about. I was ready.

We got lost. A truck driver didn't bother to tell us when we blew through Santa Fe. He dropped us off in Colorado Springs, over two hundred miles past our destination. We talked it over and decided to go on to Denver. Then we decided to go to Montana. This had been way too easy so far, so we decided to shoot for Vancouver. They love lost blind fools in Canada. T. G. and I enjoyed a non-stop party for a whole week. When we started to run low on cash, we knew it was time to head south again, back home to New Mexico. A journey of a thousand miles begins with the first step. T.G. and I walked every step of that journey together.

One day, Tokind came over to my house with a Thai Spicy Beef Salad. He said he was feeding my vision.

"What are you talking about Tom?" I asked.

"I was thinking about your vision and how you see colors. This stuff is great, it will be a real journey for you," he said. He was right, it was an explosion of color and flavor. While we were eating, Tokind asked me, "What's the deal with the Baylor Pass run? When did you do it the first time?"

"About thirty years ago, I said."

"I've walked the Baylor," he said, "I can barely imagine running it, and my eyes work fine. Why the hell would you run it? Seems like a great way to bust your ass."

"Call me crazy, but I really feel alive when I am in the midst of something big. My heart gets pumping, the sweat starts flowing, and my wind starts blowing."

"Tell me about this wind of yours George."

"You know at the start of the race, I'm just this piece of crap trying to get up the hill. But then I get my second wind, and I lose my skin and bones and become a flowing river. The current carries me away. I think if you never felt this feeling, you have never really been alive."

"So why the Baylor?" Tokind asked. "Couldn't you get this feeling running on pavement?"

"It's not the same thing at all, Tokind. There needs to be a mountain in the way. There is nothing bigger than a mountain, except me, running up that mountain. I have to strive for the second wind, or I'll never conquer any mountain."

The Dream Child: "To find truth, you must draw blood. What ever you see in the second mirror of truth, you must embrace. We all try, and sometimes we fail. There is no sin in failure. The only sin is not to try. Don't you know? The mountain is the goal. When you run up the mountain like you really mean it, you are bigger than the mountain. You are greater than your goal. Listen to me. This is the Dream Child speaking to you. Close your eyes now and tell me what you see. The mirrors of truth will set you freeeee!

I am a Freak. I am a blind fool set loose in the world. The trauma of going blind slammed me. I was smashed to smithereens, then had to glue the pieces of my life back together. Maybe it was the sports that helped me hurdle all the obstacles. In sports you train hard every day. There's blood, sweat, and sacrifices. Maybe that's part of what got me through the devastation of losing my eyesight. But I know there was a hell of a lot more than sports behind my survival, and that's what this book is about.

Before my blindness I was on top of the world. I was a star athlete. I mean championship class with real pro potential - one of the most likely to succeed in the nation. My name was on everyone's lips. My coach was beside me clapping me on the back, "You're the one, Champ."

Sports came easy for me as if I was born to win. My ability to filch a wayward ball, a basketball, football or baseball out of the air was legendary. My life as a sports hero was on cruise control. I was in with the popular crowd. I was dating a beautiful cheerleader. I said to her, "I am one happy-go-lucky man."

By the time I was fifteen the shelves in my bedroom were lined with trophies, gold silver and bronze, evidence of my countless victories, proof of my omnipotence. I was an honor roll student. I could take my pick of college scholarships. People would be throwing money at me, big, big money. I'd own hot cars. It was a set-up for glory. I would become a man of influence. I felt like Mendoza the Great.

I should have realized that something bad was happening. There was the red lettuce in my salad at dinner – not just reddish-colored leafy stuff that appears in your fancy mixed greens, but bright, blood red iceberg lettuce. I couldn't even see the full moon on a crystal clear night. Then came the recurring headaches. In basketball my accuracy slipped. I couldn't hold on to the ball. I had cement in my shoes.

I noticed my vision was fuzzy. Maybe I need glasses, I thought. Athletes are experts at denial. You deny misery and pain because you have to ignore anything that takes your mind off winning. I simply disregarded the symptoms. After all, I was strong. Hell, I was invincible. Don't be a wuss, I told myself.

The Mirrors Of Truth

In the final basketball game of the season the bleachers were packed. This was everything I'd been training for. During this final game, my world began to unravel. The ball flew straight through my outstretched hands and smashed into my face. Blood spewed from my nose. Twice in free throws, the backboard swayed in and out of focus. I missed the shots. Booed by the crowd, I, the star forward, finished my team's losing game on the bench. And that was just the beginning.

After the game my coach approached me. Coach is going to think I'm a wimp, I thought. So I said, "Bad day. I just couldn't see straight." In hindsight, those were prophetic words.

The eye doctor was an older man with a professional manner. Everything seemed routine. But I was picking up that he was very concerned by what he found in my examination. He shined a tiny probe light into my eye and asked me to look straight at it. I could not focus. The effort exhausted me. I gave up. The doctor switched on the room lights and said, "Look straight at me, George. No, into my eyes. Look directly at me."

"I am," I said. He could see that I was staring at the wall off to his left. I was getting nervous now. There were butterflies in the pit of my belly, and anxiety was expanding to my solar plexus.

Looking solemn the doctor said, "This is serious." My knees got shaky, I couldn't swallow and his voice sounded far off, muffled. He said something about how only twenty documented cases like mine existed in the world. Great, I'm a freak, I thought. The doctor said something about how my eye condition was hereditary. I remember the doctor's grave voice explaining to my mother, "George will never become a watchmaker for example, or a pilot. Still there are a great number of professional opportunities open to the blind..."

The long and short of it is I was condemned to blindness in the fifteenth year of my life. The eye doctor had found tiny, crescent-shaped lesions in the retinal layers of both of my eyes. The prognosis was for continued deterioration. I would perceive less and less light, lose my central vision and some peripheral vision, becoming legally blind.

I felt the wind-knocked-out-of-me kind of shock you feel when you jump into ice water. Sweat broke out on my forehead. I barely heard the doctor's verdict as his voice faded, as I felt my grip on reality let go.

The doctor gave my mom some information, little pamphlets I couldn't even read. I'm going blind went round in my head. I didn't say anything. My eyes misted over. My head disconnected from my body and floated up into the air, looking down on this pathetic scene. This couldn't be me. How could this happen to me?

I had no idea what it meant to be blind. I did not know anyone who was blind. Stevie Wonder and Ray Charles where the only blind people I had ever even heard of, and I wasn't gonna be a musician. There were no examples of what a blind person could do. There was nobody to tell me what I could be.

Over and over in my head went the tape loop: My athletic career is over. I'm never going to play basketball again. And I thought, I'll never drive a car. Hell, what kind of woman is going to want me now? Who's going to hang out with some cripple, some worthless guy whose life is going to hell?

My senses dulled. The world went blurry and semi-dark. The room was spinning out of control. This is my life that's just been trashed.

When I left the eye doctor's office I felt the numb sensation of receiving a death sentence. The world outside was sunny and people were moving about their daily lives. Blind? Shouldn't time stand still, meteors collide? It seemed as if my world had gone insane. The ground collapsed from under me, and I dropped into a void. It was like being buried alive. Would I die alone in this sinkhole?

Once home I opened my mouth, trying to form words and sound. What I needed to express was stuck in my throat. Finally after several attempts I said out loud to myself, "I'm going blind." Once voiced, the shock and reality of those three little words was so overwhelming I couldn't hold my emotions back. I started to cry. I cried and cried like a suffering animal. My sides ached from crying.

When I regained my composure I realized I had to accept that I would live my life blind. The doctor had spoken. My fate was sealed. I had a real nauseous feeling. I remembered being a small boy, walking home from the Garden of Eden, holding my mothers hand. There was a man with dark glasses and a ragged coat sitting on a little stool on the street corner. He held a silver cup in his hand. Propped up in front of his knees, a cardboard sign that I could not read. After we had walked further along, I asked my mother, "Who was that man? Why is he sitting there?"

My mother told me, "That man is blind Georgie. He's

begging for money."

I reflected on my mother. I, her only child, was going blind. We'd had a rough start. My father had abandoned us when I was two months old. He went out to get the Sunday morning paper and never came back. My mother had made so many sacrifices to raise me. Now I would be a blind burden. I considered the doctor's statement that my eye condition was hereditary. A relative on my dad's side had gone blind. I thought, Thanks a lot, Dad. You finally gave me something. Then thoughts that were almost unthinkable surfaced. I had built my life on athletics. Sports had given me the chance to be someone. This blindness - it wouldn't just halt my career, it would deny me my identity. Now what could I do? Who would I be if I wasn't a star athlete? A blind person making brooms?

It was as if overnight the sky fell, the gods drenched my parade. I saw no future, only dark walls. This was the cruelest act the world could throw at me. I became numb. I fell deeper and deeper into a bottomless depression. "Help," I whispered into the darkness.

Within 6 months I lost all my central vision and eighty percent of my peripheral vision. What a normal person could see at four hundred feet, I could see only within twenty feet and then only askance. Beyond the reach of my hands, colors faded to gray. I could move about without optical aids on sunny days or in bright light because of some peripheral vision. Even then it was like viewing the world through a handful of imaginary soda straws while the focus in each straw constantly changed. On hazy or overcast days I couldn't even see peripherally, so I remained indoors.

Then there was the problem of artificial light. That was like a big glaring thing in my head so I had to keep the indoor lights off. I mostly lived indoors in murky, half-light like some kind of cave creature.

If that wasn't enough, I began to get the psychedelic light show in my central vision. You may think hallucinations are cool, but you can't turn these off ever; not with your eyes open or eyes closed or when you're awake or asleep. It was hell, a never-ending nightmare. Even sounds were different, more intense. Most people can close their eyes and have some stillness. Not only was I blind, but all those insane visions put me over the top. I couldn't handle the stimulus overload. In general I couldn't sleep or if I did sleep it was fitful. I woke up startled and sweating. Sometimes I couldn't tell the difference between awake and asleep. Reality was always some dreadful half-remembered daydream or nightmare. My eyes and brain were working overtime and my brain got tired trying to unscramble signals. This caused extreme fatigue and frequent headaches. And the hundreds of eyeballs staring back at me - was I seeing the eyes of Angels? Of God? Of Spirits? Of Demons? Then a dark thought occurred to me - I might "lose it." This wasn't about just losing sports or my identity. This was madness. I could lose my mind.

Forget school. I walked around in a hopeless haze. My eyes were burned into the front of my face like brands. I kept my deteriorating vision a secret. When I refused to go out for sports, my peers called me a fink. When your glory is gone your so-called friends are gone.

Soon I was colliding with people in the school halls,

fumbling with my books. I couldn't read. I couldn't take notes. I was failing. People noticed.

I finally had to 'fess up about my debilitating condition. The kids at school would peer intently into my eyes then walk away shaking their heads. They called me "Retard" and "Reject." I didn't use a cane or wear dark glasses. I still had enough peripheral vision to remain mobile. "They" thought I was faking it, a quitter. I was humiliated to the core.

My eye-candy girlfriend told me blindness was contagious and if she kept hanging out with me she'd go blind too. So she stopped hanging out with me.

When I went to the high school counselor he took off his eyeglasses. Then he said to me, "You see, I can see just like you now." Except you can put them back on and see again, you moron, I thought.

I quit going to school. Shame and isolation were my company. I was so shut down I couldn't feel the sun or see the sky. So I quit going outside. My bedroom became my prison. Alone on my bed, I sat staring into space, waiting for something to happen, for the spinning to stop, for the movie to end, for the lights to come back up. I was a young man dying with the hours. I experienced frustration, anguish and hopelessness as if they were tangible things I could hear like sound, or feel like heat. It was as if God Himself was testing me to see how much I could endure. You won't make it, floated down from my subconscious.

Go to a school for the blind? Make brooms the rest of my life? I started to plan my suicide. So much for Mendoza the Great.

CHAPTER 3: THE THIRD MIRROR

"Little universes are everywhere."

The truth is we might all be lost. My wise friend, Tokind and I went for a LONG drive one day just to get away and talk. Nothing was going on that day so we drove up into the mountains of New Mexico. As Tokind drove me along the Black Range Mountains, I asked him jokingly if I could drive when he got tired. "George, you're blind," he said, "but I'll think about it. You probably can drive better than a lot of the people around here." We both laughed.

I first met Tokind about eight or nine years ago. I walked into his office and asked him if he could help me make a website. He agreed with a big grin on his face. The rest is history as they say. We have become very good friends! See georgemendoza.com and you'll see me.

It took us about two hours to get up to a little mountain town named Hillsboro which is a quaint peaceful place nestled in the desert foothills of the Gila Wilderness National Forest. We ate lunch at a wonderful place called The Barber Shop. After a couple of salads and sandwiches, we got back on the road. We drove about two miles when I asked Tokind to pull over at a rest stop. We parked the car and walked up into a canyon fed by a tiny creek. The sunlight was clear and strong. I could see well, which is to say well enough to walk around on my own. After we got out of the heat of the sun we stopped to collect some Mullen (which I always heard called Indian toilet paper). There was this cool moist breeze. The sunlight danced upon the treetops as I listened to the bubbling stream make its way down the valley.

"I don't understand people who need an absolute truth," Tokind told me. "For me life is all about working toward a goal. For me, my work is who I am. I work for a good life for my wife and son. I work, hard as it is sometimes, to support and do right by other people."

"That sounds good," I said. "Speak on, oh wise sage, speak your truth!"

"I go to church. I am a good Catholic. I believe in the Father, Son and the Holy Ghost. But what if Jesus was a prophet and not immortal? I mean, the teachings of Jesus work for me. When you come right down to it, it is about how to live your life in community – caring for those around you is caring for yourself. Communities learn and grow collectively. Even a herd of buffalo learn where the good water is, and what dangers to avoid. People are the most advanced expression of this idea. We learn how to remake our own world."

"Or destroy it," I said.

Tokind has this thing about mushrooms. As we walked up through the canyon he was looking at the ground. He would call me, "Hey George, come look at this." Along our walk, Tokind found all kinds of different mushrooms. Some were too small for me to really make out. Others were ears growing out of the side of dead wood. Then, he showed me this huge mushroom, as big across as a basketball. I got up real close and saw brilliant orange and yellows against a brown background.

"This could be one of your paintings," Tokind said.

"It's like a little universe," I said.

"You could use mushrooms as a theme for some of

your paintings," Tokind said.

"You know," I said, "most people I go to the woods with are, like, 'yeah there's some trees over there, some bushes.' You keep finding these little universes to look at."

"I am always looking for communities, George." Tokind remarked.

As I squatted down and touched the surface of the mushroom, this musky smell welled up. The surface was firm and warm. It actually felt like flesh.

"Feel under the rim of this thing," he said. Underneath it was cool and damp. It felt like a firm sponge. "You know," said Tokind, "there is a whole community of living under, around, and inside this thing."

"Too bad the world can't get along like this," I said.

"But I think it does, George. Whether we realize it or not, we are all bound up in this huge community. If you were far enough away, the earth looks like this organism. When you look at it, it's obvious that it is alive. I mean, it's breathing and changing over time. If you are far enough away you cannot see all of the organisms at work. But they are there."

"Constantly creating and destroying," I said, matter of factly.

"Exactly!" he said.

As we walked back to the car Tokind stopped by this really big tree. "I got another idea for you," he said.

"Shoot!" I replied, full of energy and life.

"This tree must be over a hundred years old. Once it was a seed. The design for this tree was inside that seed. Plants have very sophisticated designs for adaptation. They can't get up and move when the conditions are bad, like buffalo or people do. If a seed finds itself where there is sunlight, water, and soil, it has everything it needs to become this huge tree. But if the seed isn't nurtured, the tree will never be."

As we stood there visiting the tree, a strong hot wind blew through us, rustling the thick green leaves of the old tree. The scent of pine filled the air.

"Just look at this thing," said Tokind.

"Nice neighborhood," I said.

Tokind smiled.

The Dream Child: "Spirit Man, seeds are like ideas. They need nurturing to grow. Do you remember when Tokind showed you the mushroom as if it was earth? What if the difference between a tree and me is I have a choice about where I will be? Do you understand that design without nurture is like an empty promise? And, since we are all bound up in the same community, we are all responsible. The universe is vast, but your universe - the people and things within your grasp - are most important. People have eyes, but don't really see. We walk down the street, only worried about where we need to be. We walk past miracles every day, and we choose not to see them. Whatever you see in the third mirror of truth you must embrace. Wake up to the little universes that are all around you. This is the third mirror of truth. Listen to me. This is the Dream Child speaking to you. Close your eyes and tell me what you see. The mirrors of truth will set you freeeee!

I am a mushroom! I am a soul living in the flesh. I understand that I will die one day. But in the meantime, I have lived one helluva life!

CHAPTER 4: THE FOURTH MIRROR

"Joy is happening all around you!"

The truth is we turned around. As we walked down out of the canyon something caught our attention. Walking back up, we took another path. We came to a large rock fall and I wondered out loud, "Do you think someone did this with dynamite, or is it natural?"

Tokind answered, "It's hard to tell. I don't see any bore holes in the rock face. Sure is a big fall though." Of course, I won out when I pointed out how several huge boulders were neatly placed to stop 4-wheelers from driving up the canyon. We both laughed at the obvious.

We followed a little stream, gingerly stepping upon the smooth river boulders as we went. I followed right behind Tokind who was describing the way and the rocks to me, for which I was very grateful. He must have done a very good job describing the trail to me because the going was easy. No banged up knees or bloody lips. Tokind is the best sighted guide I've ever known.

Then he stopped all of the sudden on top of a huge rock in the middle of the stream. I almost ran into him, as I had to stop abruptly as well. "George! Check this out!" he said in a sharp breath. I saw him jump off the rock. I heard a soft thump onto deep moist earth where he landed. We were underneath some huge pine trees, all growing slanted on the northern slopes reaching toward the sun. I leaped off the same rock and landed next to Tokind, who was bowing where he stood. "Look here," he said, grabbing my arm and guiding me forward. I saw a most incredible sight.

I saw a five or six inch circle of shimmering purple-blue floating in the air, just off the ground. It was moving and shimmering like something alive, but I could not imagine what living thing it could be. Tokind pulled me back a step and told me what we were looking at. Almost breathing the words, "It's eight or nine tiny butterflies flying in a circle. None of them are bigger than a half an inch across". We watched a while, holding very still, and I noticed that the shimmering started to dissipate. "They are landing."

I saw less and less color, and then I could not see them anymore. "Where did they go?" I asked.

"They all landed" he said, "and their wings are up, so you cannot see the color now."

"Tokind," I said, "did I ever tell you about what happened to me at the Baylor pass run a couple of years ago? I was all by myself, running down through a rough spot in the canyon race when suddenly I could see a fog of colors, rising from the ground all around me. I remember hearing soft fluttering sounds, but soon the ground underneath me had disappeared. I stopped and turned all the way around to try to see what all the color was."

"What was it, George?"

"I was standing in a mist of Monarch butterflies. I think they were migrating down to Mexico. I'll never forget the experience. It is where my painting butterfly eyes came from."

As we walked on, Tokind said, "My son has been bugging me about wanting to get a bird as a pet. We love animals, but I have been explaining to him that I can't see keeping a bird as a pet unless you live in a huge cage, like the ones they have in botanical gardens." Tokind paused and then added, "Dogs are a lot like us and they fit right into our lives because they are stuck to the ground like we are, and they are social animals. They live through social relationships and depend on them for happiness."

I then asked him, "So how are birds different?"

"If you keep a bird in a cage, I don't think it's still a bird. It looks like a bird, and it might still sing, but I see birds flying. They fly alone. They fly in groups. Sometimes you see them flying up and down in the sky, diving, circling. Flocks of birds can move in perfect concert. There can be thousands of them in a flock, moving like a single living thing. Or, just two or three, diving and swooping through the air for no reason at all." Tokind paused again and then added, "I think if you take a bird away from that environment and put it in a cage, it's not the thing it was before."

"I had a friend once who had a blind parrot named George," I said. "The bird didn't move much, didn't sing. It seemed really unhappy to me."

Tokind laughed, "Did they name the Parrot after you?"

"No, that's how we were introduced."

"A blind parrot would not survive in the wild," said Tokind. "But is living in that cage any better?"

"Well, Tokind, I feel like that blind parrot in the wild," I said. "It hasn't killed me yet."

THE DREAM CHILD: "You know, Spirit Man, insects and birds live short and brutal lives. They spend all their time trying to get enough food, reproduce and then die.

But sometimes you see joy. There is no reason or motive to explain the things they do in flight. If you pay attention, joy is happening all around you! You can experience joy and even join in if you can see it, if you know what I mean. Whatever you see in the fourth mirror of truth you must embrace. Joy is the fourth mirror of truth. Listen to me. This is the Dream Child speaking to you. Close your eyes and tell me what you see. The mirrors of truth will set you freeeee!"

CHAPTER 5: THE FIFTH MIRROR

"There are two Towers in Heaven."

The truth is love is powerful and so is hate. Life is about building and destroying. I was thinking about this in my cozy little rock shelter. I was home on September 11th and the phone started ringing off the hook. I got three phone calls in a row from friends who told me to turn on the TV. They said we were being attacked. As I watched the distorted images of the airplanes flying into the buildings, it felt like a personal assault. I was born and raised in New York City. Now I've learned that just about everyone in the country felt just like I did. The destruction was personal.

Every once in a great while a person comes along in this world who knows exactly what they were born to do. Unfortunately, I was not one of those lucky people at all! Now I am almost 50 years old, and I have just figured out what I was born to do.

One day I found myself very upset and confused about the plans to rebuild the Twin Towers. Why would anyone want to build towers there again? There were people who wanted to build the towers taller than the ones before. To me, this did not make any sense. Wasn't this just asking for trouble, building a target for the terrorists to strike us once again. Then my mom showed me a political cartoon with five towers like fingers on a hand. The middle finger was tall and proud, answering the terrorists by "flipping them the bird."

I remembered a very strange dream that I had

shortly after 9/11. I wrote this story roughly three months later. My dream was crystal clear in my mind as if I was actually there in the present moment. In my dream, I the saw two towers being resurrected right in front of me in a beautiful place, which I thought must be heaven. These twin towers had all seeing eyes in them staring back at me in my dream. There was no smoke or fire coming out of the towers. No people jumping out of them. These towers stood tall and mighty. There was a fiery sun full of bright swirls of yellow and orange and red. This sun looked to me like a symbol of faith and hope in a peaceful calm blue sky.

A week later, I started painting what I thought was going to be another one of my landscapes of New Mexico where I live. I was not thinking of the dream, but as I started to paint I soon realized that this painting was going to be something different. I had just spent four hours on this painting and I had no sense of what I was doing. As I painted the background in soft blues and dark purples with white swirls, Clyde Montoya dropped by unexpectedly. Clyde has been a friend of mine for more than thirty years. As he walked into my backyard where I paint, he startled the hell out of me. I was frustrated, and stumbling around with this painting. I did not need any interruptions right now. Before Clyde came over, I was painting two tall majestic mountains in a rather large canvas. After our warm greetings to each other, Clyde got real close to my painting, studied it for a long time, and then commented, "Hey, bro! That looks like two towers to me! Good job!"

"That's it!" I shouted. I begged Clyde to stay with

me for the rest of the afternoon. He agreed with a smirk on his face.

"You can't get rid of me now!" He smiled. He sat down in a lawn chair and did not say another word. He watched me paint up a storm.

At that moment, the dream came back to me as if I were having it right then. In my mind's eye, I saw my dream about the twin towers being built in heaven. Behind them was that huge fiery sun. It had been in front of me the whole time. I just could not see it. "Towers in Heaven" would be the subject of my painting.

Clyde watched me as I painted each tower over the next two hours. Every so often Clyde would hoot, "Cool!" and cheer me on. Clyde and I go way back to the good old days at the Blind School in Alamogordo. Today, sitting in the sun 20 feet away, he could feel my excitement as I built the Towers in Heaven. When I was done I invited Clyde to look at my painting. He got up real close and studied it. "George, this is beautiful."

I realize now I was born to be a painter and a visionary despite my visual loss. Life has a funny way of taking us on a different path that we expect or even wish for. Ironically I paint what I see. Blurry visions and kaleidoscope colors that run wild in my eyes. Because of my rare eye condition I learned to see deep inside myself and not worry too much about seeing things that are outside of me. I thank God for my limitations. It turns out that they are really gifts. It also turns out that I am just like my uncle Wallace. I am here, building towers upon this earth. "This is my vision," says the Spirit Man, "to make this world a better place for you and me. When I paint, I feel closer to God. I strongly believe that if you can find something in this world to take you away from your problems for two or three hours a day, then, you have found something very magical indeed."

THE DREAM CHILD: "The whole world looked at the pile of rubble where the twin towers had fallen. We looked in horror at the destruction on our TV screens. We cried. Many gave in to the destruction. We all felt the personal assault, and many of us resigned ourselves to the horror, the hopelessness, the despair. But something beautiful happened. There were heroes there. What is a hero? A hero is somebody who does the right thing, even if it might kill him. There were so many stories of heroes on that fateful day. They did not give in to the destruction and sorrow. They did not worry about the hatred. They had a job to do. They saved lives. They helped people in need. Many died, but they changed to world forever. This is the fifth mirror of truth. Whatever you see in the fifth mirror of truth, you must embrace. Close your eyes and tell me what you see. The mirrors of truth will set you freeee!"

CHAPTER 6: THE SIXTH MIRROR

"Putting passion into your compassion."

The truth is we all need more of such moments. We need to pay more attention to the now. We need more people in the world today like my good friend, Fred Stern, a.k.a. The Rainbow Maker. I first met Fred at the World Peace Art Show at the Hal Marquez Gallery in El Paso, Texas. Fred and I were among the featured artists speaking there. Fred talked about making rainbows for peace all over the world, which I found absolutely fascinating. He had made rainbows in Israel, Washington D.C., San Francisco, and Santa Fe. He even told me a story about making a "moonbow" once for a group of kids in upstate New York who suffered from Photophobia. Fred is a man of passion.

At the show I had five rather large paintings, and I showed "Towers in Heaven" for the first time. The painting was a real hit, and more importantly the Rainbow Maker was so impressed with it that he approached me and we started talking. Fred and I became great friends. We talk about art, writing, and of course the beautiful women who run our lives.

This story is about My Beautiful Estella and how Fred Stern helped me to learn to "put a lot of passion into your compassion."

My life with Estella is a kind of wonderful dream. We have been together for over five years. Our love is perfect. She seems to understand me both as George Mendoza and as the Spirit Man! Our romance is perfect.

We traveled all over the world. We traveled to New York, Las Vegas, California, and Old Mexico. We had fun in everything that we did together! Our friendship was perfect. And she could melt me with just one kiss!

But life has a way of slapping you in your face. Your life can change dramatically in the blink of an eye. In one moment, my wonderful dream began to fall apart. The world as I knew it had been turned upside down. Estella became deathly ill. She was lying on the couch in the living room and she didn't want to get up. She told me that she did not want to live like this anymore. She told me to either call 911, or fix her a tea that would ease the pain. The next day she seemed to feel much better. The third week in July we decided to meet Tokind and his family at the Owl Bar and Cafe, in San Antonio, New Mexico, the tiny almost-ghost-town where Conrad Hilton's family opened their first hotel, with four rooms. We were going to meet there for lunch. The Owl Bar is pretty famous around these parts for a green chile cheeseburger, and the greasiest fries in the west. Men between the ages of 30 and 65 should avoid eating here more than once a year. By the time Estella and I drove the 140 miles to San Antonio, she was becoming very sick. She said she felt dizzy and weak. She was in terrific pain. Then she told me that she had been bleeding that morning.

She put on a brave face as we met our friends at the café. She hardly touched her food. She was very quiet and distant. Tokind's wife Gloria was able to talk to her a bit, but everyone could see that Estella was sick. After lunch, Gloria offered to drive for us on the way back home to Las Cruces. Estella insisted that she would be OK. They took off for Las Cruces, as I waited for Estella to rest for a few minutes in the car. Then we headed home. On the way home things got pretty scary. I talked to her the whole way, to help her stay awake. She was getting frightened at the pain and afraid that she might pass out. We had to stop several times on the way home.

The next day we went to see her family doctor. He sent us off to a specialist who agreed that she had ulcerated colitis. He told us almost nothing about it, except that the disease "waxes and wanes" and that many people go into remission for years. He prescribed anti-depressants and wished us luck.

Alone that night, I called Tokind to talk about what had happened. I told him that the doctor had prescribed an anti-depressant, and we couldn't understand why. What did this have to do with internal bleeding? He agreed that this did not make sense. The thing that confused me most was that Estella did not see anything strange about this. She just accepted the fact that the drugs would fix the problem. Tokind was asking me questions about the meeting with the doctor. He seemed to be saying that we had not asked any questions, or that we asked the wrong questions. Tokind said that there was something missing. Something the doctor did not want to tell us. He told me I should get a second opinion.

Looking back on things now, she almost died several times on my watch during that long hot summer. By the end of July, after many weeks in and out of doctors' offices, visits to hospitals, and numerous tests, we didn't know anything more than we knew at that first visit to the family doctor. For six months, Estella lost a lot of blood because she was bleeding internally. She became very weak, tired, severely depressed and anemic. She lost fifteen pounds in three weeks. She became very dizzy because of the large loss of blood. She could no longer drive.

Still Estella was insisting that she would be going back to school to teach in a few weeks, and that she was going to continue her masters program at the University. Here I was looking at a woman who was so sick that she could not walk out of the house, insisting that nothing had changed. Part of me thought, what a brave sweet child. Another part of me thought, this is madness.

She would sleep all day and would not leave the living room couch unless she had to go to the bathroom. She was going to the bathroom twenty times a day. I tried to talk to her, to figure out what I could do to help her. The Estella that I knew and that I was madly in love with was always bright eyed and happy and full of life. How could I help her to be that person again? I saw this beautiful woman, my Estella, wasting away in front of me. I remember crying alone every night, agonizing over what I was going to do. Estella had moved into the other bedroom. She said that any movement in the bed would wake her with terrific pain.

She could not eat anything without going to the bathroom. She would bloat up with gas, and run to the bathroom in the middle of dinner. She was eating so little that I feared for her life. One look at her pale sick face and thin body would tell anyone that there was no way that she was going to make it back to work by early August. But she did not see it that way.

By now, I was desperate. Her health was failing and I felt completely helpless. What was I going to do for Estella? Hell, I was blind! I couldn't even drive her to her doctors' appointments. How was I going to help her. I was paralyzed with my own fear. That is when I called Fred and asked him if we could get together as soon as possible.

The next morning Fred came over. He found me in my office, sitting in my chair, staring off in to space. Fred took the other chair and he just listened as I poured it all out. I told him what I knew about Estella's condition, and that I was sure she was going to die right there in my house. I told him that she had explained that her grandmother and two of her aunts had died from this same condition.

I told him I could not handle all of this. I was so anxious with my fear. I knew that I could no longer take care of her. I told Fred that I was useless to her. I couldn't take her to her doctors appointments. I couldn't take her to the pharmacy to get medicine. I wasn't qualified to be her caregiver. I couldn't handle the idea of her dying in my arms.

Fred shifted his weight in the chair, and did not say anything. Then I started demanding answers of him. What the hell was I going to do? Would I have to commit her to the hospital? Would I have put her in a resting home? I couldn't handle this. But if I did not take care of her, who would? The thought of abandoning her at this time made me feel so sad. All my life people took care of me. My mother took care of me when I was a child. Estella took care of me for the first five years of our loving relationship. But now the tables had turned. I knew that there was no way I could take care of my beautiful Estella.

Again the Rainbow Maker shifted his weight in his chair. For a minute or so he didn't say anything. "George, you're so full of shit. You don't know if she is going to die or not. You've made up this whole tragic story. You don't know how this story is going to end. You don't even know what's going to happen tomorrow." Then he stood up. He said "You need to crawl out of your own ass. All you need to worry about is what you are going to do today. You don't think you can do the right thing? Just love her. Listen to her. Make her a good soup."

This wasn't the answer I had been looking for. Now I really felt trapped. Again I insisted, "there is no way I can deal with this Fred. The doctor said that the disease is chronic." I opened my mouth to protest some more, but Fred was already walking out the door. The door slammed shut. I sat there in my chair, alone again. I sat there for hours, staring now at a blank canvas. I started to shed the paralyzing fear. Maybe Fred was right. Maybe I could help Estella. Was this really so different than the challenges I had faced before? What if I just took care of the moment? All I had to do was to make dinner, take her outside to watch the beautiful New Mexico sunset, and tell her how much I loved her. I could do this.

And that's what I did! The Spirit man inside me went to the kitchen and made Estella a tea.

The Dream Child: "Spirit Man, you know that you can fill that blank canvas with paint, and make it your own vision. This is no different than the commitment you make before that blank canvas. Estella has been your friend, your companion, your Spirit woman for many years. Fred is a true friend. There are times when you must lose yourself, and the weight of the world, and take care of the moment. You know that you can keep the commitment you share with Estella. Taking care of somebody you love when the mirror begins to crack is the sixth mirror of truth. Whatever you see in the sixth mirror of truth you must embrace. Close your eyes and tell me what you see. The mirrors of truth will set you freeee!"

CHAPTER 7: THE SEVENTH MIRROR

"The Angel who flew away."

The truth is there are real mirrors and there are dead mirrors. When you get up in the morning to clean up and get ready for the day, the mirror that you are looking at is dead. It only reflects the image of your face. The real mirrors in your life are the people you love, the people you live with, and the people you work with. They are your real mirrors, and you are a reflection of their lives as well. The dead mirror can deceive you. Vanity is an empty image. As I walk out of the bathroom, I don't say goodbye to the mirror hanging there. I walk into the kitchen to find Estella there. The coffee smells good to me but her warm hug every morning is what means the most to me. This is a real mirror. My love and friendship with her is a fulfilling image.

Do you understand the mirrors in your life? Do you cherish them? Do you value them? Or, do you stop looking when you walk away from the dead mirror in your bathroom? The reflection of your real place in this world is in the faces of the people around you. And these people are counting on you.

Listen to me now! The Real Mirrors of Truth: We live in a sea of skin and bones. We pretend that our bodies and our faces are who we really are. These are the images in the dead mirror. A shape. A form. An illusion. A ghostly image at best. You and I are stranded in that sea of skin and bones. It's like this, my sighted fool wonder! You are, most important, a mirror reflecting everything that you see and feel all around you in the world. You are a real mirror walking down a busy street. As you swim through the sea of skin and bones, the people all around you don't see you because they are too busy looking at their own reflections.

There is only one dead mirror. Every mirror that hangs on a wall is the same mirror. We do not look at that mirror to admire it. We only look for some reflection of ourselves. That reflection is not who we are. Look around you! Real mirrors are everywhere! I am a mirror of simple truths. You are a mirror of simple truths. Look me in the eye. I am looking back at you. We can love one another or stand in the dark shadows of a mirror of hate. Love or hate. Light or darkness. We choose. I hope you choose to shine. Let your mirror reflect love and kindness to everyone around you. Shine on, my brothers and sisters. Shine on!

The Real Mirrors of Truth: When Joey died, his parents, brothers, sisters, aunts and uncles cried. My cousin Joey was five years old when he died of Leukemia. The whole family gathered at his funeral. On his casket was a picture of Joey with the angelic smile that he wore all the time. We carry pictures in our wallets. We carry pictures in our minds. On that day, Joey's bright life and heart warming smile was forever stamped in our hearts. As long as I live, Joey's living mirror is a part of my life.

The Real Mirrors of Truth: We are here one day and gone the next. We are like a vapor made of tiny atoms put together. For what, sixty years or so? Joey's skin and bones are buried in the ground, but Joey is not really dead. I still see his smile whenever I think of him.

The Real Mirrors of Truth: T.G. Gibbs died in a terrible motorcycle accident on a lonely highway in New Mexico. I met T.G. in 1973 at the New Mexico School for the Blind. T.G. was the wild cowboy who had challenged me and taunted me when I was feeling sorry for myself with no hope in sight. He dragged me, kicking and screaming, out of the dark hole I was hiding in. He opened my eyes. We became lifelong friends. I was hitchhiking up to northern New Mexico to see him, and I stopped to see Tim Kailey in Albuquerque.

"Didn't you hear?" he said. "T.G. died in a motorcycle accident a few days ago." Puff! We all go up in smoke! T.G. was 19 years old, almost totally blind, headed down a highway at 75 miles per hour, on a motorcycle.

"God damn him!" I cursed, when I found myself grieving, and angry for his having been so careless. Here one day and then gone. Gone in a split second! I was taking it very personally, as though he had taken something very valuable away from me. I suddenly realized that in being angry about what I had lost, I began to see how valuable he really had been in my life. Bam, there was the mirror. I had to ask myself, "If I were gone tomorrow, what valuable thing would I be taking away from the people who know me?"

The Real Mirrors of Truth: Estella left. Her family came and helped her pack up her belongings. When I came back to the house one day, it was empty. My angel was gone. I don't know why she flew away. I walked through my empty house. It didn't feel like a home to me anymore. My most cherished mirror had vanished. The kitchen the table and four chairs, the bed, all of the material things in the house could burn. These things are not important to me. My angel is. My beautiful Estella, my lovely angel, had flown away. We had reached a point where she couldn't help me, and I couldn't help her. That was the truth we both didn't want to face. The world is a hard place, and there are conditions that even the greatest love you can feel will not change.

The Real Mirrors of Truth: One minute you are happy in your life and then something terrible happens to you. "Yeah, in the single beat of a heart," says the man in the mirror. "We are fragile beyond words. I want you to stand in front of your mirror right now. Even though you can't see your heart beating inside your chest, it is pumping blood into your veins. Its beat gives you life so you can think and dream and run and love and dream all over again. As long as your heart beats, it will hurt. We all bleed, brothers and sisters. Otherwise we're all dead. I want you to look into the mirror, Spirit Man! Look upon its smooth face! What do you see? Do you see yourself? I am going to throw a rock at your reflection in that mirror. Right now, I am going to smash you beyond recognition, Spirit Man! I am going to destroy your life until you exist no more. I am not even going to feel sorry for you, Spirit Man! You must not cling to or hold onto anything at all, Spirit Man! I am here to set you freeeee! Your mirror has been broken into millions of pieces. Broken glass is flying all over the place. Your image is destroyed, ha ha ha! Are you no longer there now, Spirit Man?"

The Real Mirrors of Truth: I am a mortal man. I cannot fly: I spent several weeks trying to understand why my angel flew away. I asked myself what I had said, what I had done. Did I drive her away? I asked myself over and over again. And then I asked my mother. I asked my friends. I left my empty house. A dear friend of mine offered to shelter me for a while. There, I poured out all of my pain, anger, and disappointment onto paper. My mother and my friends circled around me. They didn't want me to fall apart. They wanted to help me get over the angel who flew away.

One night my friend Chef picked me up. "We're going to a party," he said. We went to a pecan orchard down in the valley. It was cold and clear. There was a fire and a circle of friends under the moonlit New Mexico sky. We talked and laughed and smoked and drank. There were guitars and we were singing around the fire. Just then I was feeling a little better about my life. A snow flake landed on my cheek. I looked up through the dark naked branches of the pecan trees to see a brilliant white moon, with a ring of ice around it. The snowflakes were falling from a clear sky. I chose the light over the darkness. It was a sad thing when innocent little Joey died. I keep a picture of him in my heart. When T.G. died, I was angry at him for being so careless with his precious life, and with his friendship to me. But when my angel flew away I had to accept that I was helpless to bring her back.

In a dream I saw Estella smiling at me, reaching for my hand. When I moved forward to touch her the image shattered into millions of pieces and flew away. I woke up from this haunting dream alone, in the dark. I cried until the sun rose. I called her name in my empty house, but there was no answer.

"The truth is I miss you, My Beautiful Estella. I am

in so much pain living without you that I cannot see. The vision is gone."

What is an angel? My angel is the one I love. My angel is the one I hold in my arms. Her laughter fills up my soul with joy. Her smile is like a little sunrise even when it is dark. Her embrace is the most comfortable place in the world. My Beautiful Estella is my angel. Estella would tell me, "I want you to write a book. Write a book that will help everyone, because that is a great book. Then write another one. And write another one after that." She told me, "Every time you go out to paint in the back yard, paint a masterpiece. Fill it up with your eyes, and suns, and dreams." Estella thought that everything I did was wonderful and she always asked me to do more. And that is exactly what I was going to do.

There had always been another side to my dream life with Estella. There was something about her passions that always felt a little strange. Estella was always trying to improve everything. We were working on the yard. We were working on the house. She would insist on changing things that did not seem very important to me. One day I thought, "This is becoming a pain in the ass! Nothing here is good enough for her." I was helping her put together her own office in the spare bedroom. The day she came home and slammed the door to her office, I waited for her to come back out. I called to her. She didn't answer. Then there was a banging noise. I pushed the door open as she was hanging a mirror on the wall. We had bought the mirror months before and I had not seen it since. I saw the reflection from the window on the mirror as she stepped back to look at what she had done. "There," she said.

Then my angel flew away. If I had wings, I would fly after her and get her back. I am but a mortal man. My feet are stuck here on the ground. I can run like the wind but I cannot fly. I would do anything to bring my angel back, but now she is long gone. It does not really matter why she left. It does not really matter how far away she went. All I can say is that she is gone. She is gone and I am so sad and lonely. A dear friend of mine once told me that my heart will mend one day, but this is hard for me to accept. Time does not heal all wounds. Some people choose to pick at their wounds. Those wounds never heal. Those people never heal. Somehow people allow the wounds to heal, but we are left with scars. In a way, our lives are a collection of scars. Healing the past does not change it.

I am a very lucky man. I was blessed by knowing her, my angel. One day Estella told me, "You are the only man in the whole wide world who was able to unlock the golden lock around my heart. I love you!" The special gifts that came from her heart taught me more than you will ever know. I n losing her, I had learned that I could care so much for someone that I could forget myself, and commit myself to caring for her. Even though the loss brings pain, it was still the most wonderful thing I had done at that moment, and the most wonderful feeling I had ever known. This is the angel I will keep. This is the picture I choose to carry, stamped on my heart.

The Dream Child: "You see, Spirit Man, all angels fly away. Every body dies. Every Spirit lives. As the pieces of broken mirror spiral across Space and Time, all that remains are the real mirrors. As the skin and bones rot away in the ground, all that really matters is how you lived your life. This is the Seventh mirror of truth. Whatever you see in the Seventh mirror of truth you must embrace. All angels fly away. Joey's mirror was shattered. T.G.s mirror was shattered. Estella's mirror was shattered. Before I shatter all of your mirrors, you must understand two things. You must give to others as much as you can of yourself, and you must learn how to love as much as you can. If you take from others, and do not give, if you choose darkness over the light, then you have learned nothing and have done much harm both to yourself and to the world. Love is why we are here. Hate gets us nowhere. "You choose, Spirit Man. You choose the pictures to stamp on your heart. Each image is a gift from life. You must pick up the pieces of these broken mirrors and put them to-gether. Do you see the cracks in the mirror? That's life. A so-called perfect mirror is dead. It reflects only your illusion, the skin and bones. We only dance and smile upon this earth for a very short time. Embrace the real mirrors of truth. Cherish every gift that life gives you. Use these angels to build your perfect mirror. Your mirror of truth. As the blood flows, so does the love flow like a river through your veins. Close your eyes and tell me what you see! The mirrors of truth will set you freeeee!"

CHAPTER 8: THE EIGHTH MIRROR

"I can't see a damn thing!"

The truth is that only believing your own eyes is a kind of blindness. When it comes to vision, your eyesight is not the whole picture. My Mom likes to joke about Tokind and me getting together on Fridays to solve the problems of the world. What we really do is cook and eat and drink a beer and talk about what is important in our lives. We are friends. And this means that we trust each other. We listen to each other. We share our interests and respect each other's lives. And, we haven't figured out a damn thing!

Tokind and I both have sons. His son is 12 years old now and he tells me stories about things they do and conversations they have. I like hanging around with Arthur too, because he is like almost any boy his age. He says whatever is on his mind, and he is only interested in your response to him. Tokind says that boys from age four to thirty-five all operate on one simple principle. "Run it up the flagpole and see who salutes." I always chuckle when Tokind says this. I see myself on a big green hill, running a flag up a pole and waiting for the applause. Kids are fun because everything is brand new to them. If you play your cards right, you get to relive some of those old wonders through fresh young eyes. That is, if you are a true friend.

My son Michael wanted to be athletic, like his dad. He was in soccer, little league baseball, basketball, wrestling, and track. He played in all of these sports but he was never happy with his performance. "I suck at this! I hate it!" he would say. His basketball team was winless, and he could not hit a baseball. His mother would tell him it was OK to quit. But he was listening to me, so I encouraged him to keep trying.

When he was twelve he got an A on an essay he wrote for school, which he titled "Winners never Quit, Quitters never Win." I told him that quote from a banner that hung in my high school gym. As I went blind that banner had faded from my view. For a couple of years there, I was a quitter. I was lost. But you know what? Those words never left me. And I had to live them all over again for my great friend, my son, Michael. When I sucked, when I hated my life, I did not have a father to look to. My mom did her best, but no mother, no matter how strong, no matter how much she cares, can be a father. I was determined to be a father, and a friend, to Michael. Michael never was a quitter. He dug deep within himself and even though he was not destined to be an athlete, he is a very bright and determined young man. A man with a bright future. He is doing great at the University, and has done summer internships in Washington DC. He wants to serve the people. He wants to work in government. I'm very proud of him.

Last week Tokind and I got together and decided to go for a ride. There is a beautiful park here called Young Park. We walked around the little lake a few times and talked. Tokind was telling me about his night blindness. "Sometimes I scare the hell out of myself driving at night. I have to be really careful or I will end up running up onto a curb or a median strip. It's like the glare from the streetlights and other headlights blinds me. I can't see worth a shit." I laughed at this. "Next time you need a nighttime chauffer, you just give me a holler, Tokind."

We sat down on a stone bench looking out on the lake. I could see the glimmer of light reflecting off of the waves, flashing in our eyes. Suddenly Tokind said, "Look George! There's a red tailed hawk, hovering up there on the breeze." As we both looked up, all I could see was the sun.

"Where is it Tokind?"

"It's right there, in front of the sun," he said.

All I could see was intense white light, and then pulsing waves of color. Then it occurred to me that after a few seconds of staring right into the sun, that is probably just what it looked like to Tokind too. In a way we were both experiencing the same thing, living in the same unreal world.

All of the sudden that light passed through us like a blast from a time travel ray gun, and we found ourselves in another place. There were colors all around us, bright and swirling.

"I can't see a damned thing George, where are we?" Tokind sounded frightened.

I knew exactly where we were. We were sitting at the exact center of Tokind Tower. I had discovered this old abandoned water tower on Bob Browning's Ranch on the huge flat desert plains of the four corners area of New Mexico. The tower is no longer used as a water tank. There is a big hole in the top of it. Kids have, over the years, brought old furniture and mattresses here to make it a secret party place. Here's the thing: there are mirrors stuck to the walls all over the inside of this tank. That is why I named it Tokind tower. There are mirrors everywhere, shards of mirrors, whole mirrors, round mirrors, and big rectangular mirrors covering the inside. When the noonday sun pours into this place, it is so bright you would think you were standing out under the sun, but it's very cool inside.

We were sitting there exactly at noon, and the light was all red and orange, like the sun was setting. We heard a strong wind howling outside, but it was perfectly still where we were sitting. Suddenly Tokind jumped up and managed to smack me in the head, which really pissed me off. "What's wrong with you?" I hollered out.

He hollered right back at me. "This shit is not funny George. I can't see! Where the hell are we?"

"Hold it, Tokind," I scolded him. "Before you smack me in the head again, you gotta calm down and listen. I know where we are." I could hear Tokind breathing hard, like we had just climbed up Tortugas. "Welcome to my world!" I said.

Suddenly I saw a bright flash of light. A moment later a thunderclap told me what this was. Tokind's voice quivered. "I smell ozone George."

"It's a storm blowing in," I told him. " Stick close to me." I reached out for his arm. He was shaking. Then there was a huge explosion of brilliant colors in front of us. The kaleidoscope sea of colors hovered above us in the middle of the tower. I could see pinwheels in the sky, zigzags, trapezoids, lightning bolts, and rays of the sun spinning around and around in the middle of the fog of colors. I saw the moon turning into blood and snow blowing black. All hell was breaking loose around us, and Tokind was not a happy camper. He clutched at my arm and I thought he was going to start climbing up me like a tree.

"George," he screamed, "you gotta tell me what the hell is happening here."

"The Mirrors of Truth!" I said.

Rain began pouring in through the top of the tower. I started to step away from the center, but Tokind was frozen in fear. "Follow me," I barked over the sound of the driving rain.

His grip relaxed a little. "OK" he said. I led Tokind out of the rain to the west wall of the tower. The light was a little stronger there.

There in the waning light of a setting sun, the wind howling all around us, rain pouring into the top of Tokind tower, the mirrors began to dance before our eyes. "Tell me what you see," I said.

"George, I told you, I can't see shit!"

"Close your eyes," I said. "Relax. Don't try to look. Just wait and see."

We heard the wind blowing even harder. The tower became like a bottle, and The Great Spirit blew over the top of that bottle so that a single pure note vibrated through us. The light show continued, and I could hear whispers in the sounds all around us.

"George," said Tokind, "I see colors. I see light like it is shimmering off of mirrors. I see eyes. Is this what it is like for you?"

"Yes," I said.

Tokind was calm now. "Are the mirrors real, George? Or is this all just in my head?"

"We're on this trip together, Tokind. These mirrors are as real as you and I."

"Does that mean we see the same thing?" he asked.

"Of course not," I said. "Your vision is unique to you. No one else sees the way you do, Tokind. Just like no one else in the world sees like me."

Then, just as suddenly, the wind dropped off, and the tower faded away, and there we were sitting on that stone bench, looking out over the lake at Young Park. There was a cool breeze and some clouds were blowing in.

"Smells like rain," said Tokind.

"Lets go get some lunch," I said.

"Good idea." he said.

THE DREAM CHILD: "Spirit Man, you had the strength to take your friend Tokind by the hand, and lead him to a better place. You led him out of the storm to shelter. Tokind felt your strength and confidence, and so he followed you to a place where he could finally see. Are you the same pilgrim who began this journey? When Wallace died you saw nothing but failure and pain. The path was hard. You were looking for someone to follow. Today you ARE someone to follow. At the beginning of your journey you were just a man of limited eyesight. Today you are a man of unlimited vision. Whatever you see in the eighth mirror of truth you must embrace. Being a friend is not about what you take, it is about giving of yourself. Offering your best, especially in the dark times, is the mark of true friendship. This friendship is it's own reward. Sebastian Spirit Man! Listen to me! This is The Dream Child speaking to you! Close your eyes now and tell me what you see! The Mirrors of Truth will set you freeeeee!"

I am a man of limited eyesight, but I have unlimited vision!

CHAPTER 9: THE NINTH MIRROR

"The mirror found"

The truth is life is a blank canvas. You can leave it white or put your mark on it. I choose to paint a masterpiece on the raw canvas that has been given to me. I may not be any more a master artist than the elephants and apes who paint pictures, but that is still the way I want to feel about what I do. I don't know what my next picture will look like yet, but it will be a masterpiece, my best ever. What picture are you going to paint on your blank canvas? I hope it's a beautiful one!

As I sit here on top of the mountain, the sun is setting and dusk is slowly creeping over the land. Any sunset has a kind of silence to it, no matter what is going on. But as I listen there are sounds, faint and gentle, all around me. I feel the first breath of cool air, relief from the yellow-hot sun of the desert day. I smell the faint odor of the desert dust, raining down out of the atmosphere as the air cools. The rock walls of my special place have been soaking up the hot rays of the sun all day long. Now I feel the heat of these walls, letting go the warmth of the fiery sun. As the light turns orange, amber, then red, I sense these walls catching fire.

The Great Spirit of the Wind and Mountains dances before me in a long flowing robe of white feathers. Distant sounds of ancient flutes fill the air as the Great Spirit turns to face me. I feel as sense of shock and wonder as I see this face for the first time. The face of the Great Spirit is that of an old man. I see the deep crags of the desert mountains in the wrinkles of this face. I see the fiery oranges, ambers, and reds of the desert in the weathered skin of this face. Then I look for the eyes of the Great Spirit but there are none. Where I should see eyes, there are only deep dark pools. "Is The Great Spirit blind?" I wondered silently to myself.

The Great Spirit faces me in silence. A hand reaches out to me. In this hand is a small object. As I reach out to accept this gift from the Great Spirit, I hear a loud clap and then the spirit is gone. A shower of pebbles falls to the ground at my feet. I reach down and pick up one of the pebbles. It is cold in my hand. As I toss the pebble to the ground, I realize that I can no longer see. The sun has gone to warm up another part of the earth. The cool soft breeze of an enchanted New Mexico night is all around me. The object in my hand is a disk of cool hard plastic. It is like a clam shell, but without ridges. As I fiddle around with the object in the darkness, I find a tiny latch. With a snap the object opens up. A cold white light fills my eyes and the darkness is gone.

In my vision I am a boy running through the woods of New York with my friends, Bobby Cook and Neal Hidalgo. There is a bright white full moon shining over our heads. I have been on this path before. We are headed to a place we call The Snake Pit. It is a spooky place underneath a small bridge that runs over a country road. It is a dark and damp place, spooky as hell in the cold night. Neal has brought a candle, and somebody brings out a book of matches. I light a match and touch it to the wick of the candle in Neal's hand. The candle lights the walls and we see graffiti spray-painted all over the place. "Sally + Mike forever," one declared. "For a good time, call Juicy Lucy 555-0142." Then there it was. Those three haunting, mind boggling, life changing words. Someone had white-washed a shoebox sized section of the wall. Red letters asked, "Find What Truth?"

Then the darkness returned. I heard a voice in the darkness. "Hey, George, you there?" It was Tokind.

"Yeah," I said, "I'm right over here."

He was panting heavily from the effort of climbing up Tortugas to find me. "I was sure you would be here, George. If it wasn't for this big full moon, you would have been on your own tonight."

I took his hand. "I'm ready to go home Tom," I said. Tokind reached down for my backpack, resting against the rock wall. I stopped him, and I handed him the Clam shell.

"What's this," Tokind asked me.

"It's a long story," I said. "Lets just get off this mountain, what do you say?"

Tokind helped me slings the backpack onto my shoulders, and he slipped the clamshell into his pocket. Together we walked in silence down the mountain, a long trip just enjoying each other's company. The air around us grew warmer as we descended to the floor of the desert. Tokind's truck was parked there. Tokind tossed the backpack into the bed of his truck, and unlocked the doors.

"Look, George. The moon is hanging right over the dome of Tortugas. The moon is catching a ride on the back of the turtle."

"Yeah," I said. "I'm beat, how about I catch a ride with you?"

About thirty minutes later, we pulled up to my house.

"I'm done for today, Tokind," I said with a sigh. "Thanks for the ride." I got out of the truck and headed for my door.

"Hey, what about your backpack?" he called out.

"Right," I said. "There is something in it I'd like you to have."

"So what's in it?" he asked.

"Some stories I have been working on." He knows I write by talking to my computer. "I printed this out for you."

"What is it?" he asked.

"The Mirrors of Truth," I said with a big happy grin. "You are the first in the whole world to see them, my dear friend Tommy Spirit Man. I'm looking forward to seeing what you will do with them."

IN CLOSING, IMAGINE.

The DREAM CHILD: "Dive deep into your inner mind and tell me what you find there. You must strengthen your body, mind, and soul as one, to be a force in this world. I tell you this, oh Spirit of Man, if the body is weak, it makes the mind and spirit weak as well. It is very rare indeed for one of the three natural forces in man to have become weakened and the others to work together. That is why we have so many sick people in the world. Unfortunately, few of them overcome their woes. You, my friend are the exception to the rule because you are a long distance runner. That is why you have been able to accomplish so much with your life despite so much adversity, because you are prepared for the long haul, not just the sprinter's burst of effort.

"You have also been blessed with the God given talents to lecture and write and paint. I want you to paint the visions that I have given you in your mind when you close your eyes, and I want you to write all of this down in a little book. John Lennon had it right, Spirit Man. The best thing that you can do to change the world for the better is to use your imagination! 'Imagine there's no Heaven; it's easy if you try; no Hell below us, above us only sky. Imagine all the people, living for today...'"

The Mirrors Of Truth

"I didn't know you were a Beatle fan!" I laughed.

"I can't stand that sissy Paul, but I sure do admire the hell out of that Johnny boy," said Dream Child enthusiastically. "Don't be foolish and blind to your imagination. Imagination is how you get from here to there, no matter where you choose to go. When you use your imagination, and make a choice that you would like something to be better, then you have a dream. Follow your dreams no matter how difficult the journey becomes. When you face your problems, and we all have our share of them, you must attack them like a fierce warrior doing battle. Never think of defeat or despair, Spirit Man! Always picture triumph in your mind's eye. Even if you don't win every battle, as long as you know that you gave it your best shot, then you are still a winner to me. The journey is much more important than the destination, so you might as well enjoy yourself along the way.

"One more thing before I go, Spirit Man. The world has eyes, but IT sees not. We see things in the world for what they are, and we are thereby enabled to see what they can become. Rub your forehead, Spirit Man, and visualize the Third Eye there, the one that can see what the other two cannot. We all have one, you know. We just have to find it and use it once in a while. Open your mind as wide as you can, and don't rely too much on your eyesight. Listen to me! This is The Dream Child speaking to you! Close your eyes and tell me what you see! The Mirrors of Truth will set you freeeee!"

With that said and done, the Dream Child disappeared in a puff of sparkling hummingbird fluff, and the vision was gone.

I hope you will come to visit me someday up on the top of Tortugas mountain, where I sit by the little shrine that has been here so long, and I pick up the things people have put there, and I can see their stories and feel their hearts. Don't worry when you come. There is a part of me that will always be here, and I will be waiting just for you.

THE END

THE AUTHOR

George Mendoza was raised by his mother in New York until as a promising teenage athlete, he lost his vision to a rare disease which left him not without the sensations of sight, but living in a bizarre and surreal world of blobs and flashes of color. At the New Mexico School For The Visually Handicapped, he became a champion blind runner, and he received medals in the Handicapped Olympics in New York and Holland in 1980 and 1984. He began writing in 1982, while working on the PBS-TV documentary about his life, hosted by Robert Duvall. Working with James and others, he began the projects that eventually became the screenplay and novel "A Vision Of Courage," the screenplay "W.I.S.H." and finally, "Spirit Man." Most recently, George has discovered he can use his distorted vision to create images on canvas which he says resemble the world as he sees it, and which also reflect something of his inner world as well. He has produced dozens of paintings which have been seen in numerous galleries on tour, earning him a growing reputation as an artist.

www.georgemendoza.com

The Mirrors Of Truth